This Quilt Journal Belongs To

_____

_____

_____

Let's Get Started

Date: _____

Who is my quilt for? _____

Why am I making this quilt - will I keep it or gift it? _____

Who will I gift it to? _____

What size quilt?   Baby   Twin   Queen   King   Cal King

What is the Pattern Name, if any ? _____

What colors do I want to use? _____

What pattern(s) will I use? _____

What type of batting will I use? _____

Will I hand quilt, machine quilt or hire someone to quilt? _____

Notes: _____
_____
_____
_____
_____
_____
_____
_____
_____
_____
_____
_____
_____
_____
_____
_____
_____

Tables to Help You Calculate Yardage

Keep These Tips In Mind:

Most Quilt Fabrics are 45" wide with about 40" usable.

Divide number of total inches by 36 (number of inches in a yard) to get the number of yards. Add additional yardage to cover for errors.

Don't forget about your binding yardage.

Conversion Decimal to Fraction

Decimal	Fraction
.0625	1/16
.125	1/8
.1875	3/16
.25	1/4
.3125	5/16
.4375	7/16
.5	1/2
.5625	9/16
.625	5/8
.666	2/3
.6875	11/16
.75	3/4
.8125	13/16
.875	7/8
.9375	15/16

Standard Bed Sizes

Bed	Dimensions Inches	Quilt with 16" drop on each side	Std. Batting Sizes
Crib	28" X 52"	60" X 84"	45" X 60"
Twin	39" X 75"	71" X 107"	72" X 90"
Long Twin	39" X 80"	71" X 112"	----------
Full	54" X 75"	86" X 107"	81" x 96"
Queen	60" X 80"	92" X 112"	90" X 108"
King	76" X 80"	108" X 112"	120" X 120"
California King	72" X 84"	104" X 116"	120" X 120"

Notes

Fabric Swatches and Yardage:

Name of Fabric: _____

Cost Per Yard: _____

Notes: _____

Name of Fabric: _____

Cost Per Yard: _____

Notes: _____

Name of Fabric: _____

Cost Per Yard: _____

Notes: _____

Name of Fabric: _____

Cost Per Yard: _____

Notes: _____

Fabric Swatches and Yardage:

Name of Fabric: _____

Cost Per Yard: _____

Notes: _____

Name of Fabric: _____

Cost Per Yard: _____

Notes: _____

Name of Fabric: _____

Cost Per Yard: _____

Notes: _____

Name of Fabric: _____

Cost Per Yard: _____

Notes: _____

Materials Needed

FABRICS:

Face Fabric: _____
    Light: _____
    Medium: _____
    Dark: _____
Muslin / Backing _____
Binding/Sashing to Go Around Edges _____

THREAD NEEDED:

Color: _____
Size and Number Spools: _____
_____
Color: _____
Size and Number Spools: _____
_____
Color: _____
Size and Number Spools: _____

BATTING NEEDED:

Size: _____

OTHER MATERIALS:

_____
_____
_____
_____
_____
_____
_____
_____
_____
_____

Quilt History

Project / Quilt Name: —————————————————————

Date Quilt Top Was Started: —————————————————

Date Quilt Top Was Completed: ————————————————

How Was It Quilted and by whom: ———————————————

Date Quilt was Completed: ————————————————————

—————————————————————————————————————

PHOTO OF THE FINISHED QUILT

Let's Get Started

Date: _____

Who is my quilt for? _____

Why am I making this quilt - will I keep it or gift it? _____

Who will I gift it to? _____

What size quilt?   Baby   Twin   Queen   King   Cal King

What is the Pattern Name, if any ? _____

What colors do I want to use? _____

What pattern(s) will I use? _____

What type of batting will I use? _____

Will I hand quilt, machine quilt or hire someone to quilt? _____

Notes: _____
_____
_____
_____
_____
_____
_____
_____
_____
_____
_____
_____
_____
_____
_____

Tables to Help You Calculate Yardage

Keep These Tips In Mind:

Most Quilt Fabrics are 45" wide with about 40" usable.

Divide number of total inches by 36 (number of inches in a yard) to get the number of yards. Add additional yardage to cover for errors.

Don't forget about your binding yardage.

Conversion Decimal to Fraction

Decimal	Fraction
.0625	1/16
.125	1/8
.1875	3/16
.25	1/4
.3125	5/16
.4375	7/16
.5	1/2
.5625	9/16
.625	5/8
.666	2/3
.6875	11/16
.75	3/4
.8125	13/16
.875	7/8
.9375	15/16

Standard Bed Sizes

Bed	Dimensions Inches	Quilt with 16" drop on each side	Std. Batting Sizes
Crib	28" X 52"	60" X 84"	45" X 60"
Twin	39" X 75"	71" X 107"	72" X 90"
Long Twin	39" X 80"	71" X 112"	----------
Full	54" X 75"	86" X 107"	81" x 96"
Queen	60" X 80"	92" X 112"	90" X 108"
King	76" X 80"	108" X 112"	120" X 120"
California King	72" X 84"	104" X 116"	120" X 120"

Notes

Fabric Swatches and Yardage:

Name of Fabric: _____

Cost Per Yard: _____

Notes: _____

Name of Fabric: _____

Cost Per Yard: _____

Notes: _____

Name of Fabric: _____

Cost Per Yard: _____

Notes: _____

Name of Fabric: _____

Cost Per Yard: _____

Notes: _____

Fabric Swatches and Yardage:

Name of Fabric: _____

Cost Per Yard: _____

Notes: _____

Name of Fabric: _____

Cost Per Yard: _____

Notes: _____

Name of Fabric: _____

Cost Per Yard: _____

Notes: _____

Name of Fabric: _____

Cost Per Yard: _____

Notes: _____

Materials Needed

FABRICS:

    Face Fabric: _____

        Light: _____

        Medium: _____

        Dark: _____

    Muslin / Backing _____

    Binding/Sashing to Go Around Edges _____

THREAD NEEDED:

    Color: _____

    Size and Number Spools: _____

    _____

    Color: _____

    Size and Number Spools: _____

    _____

    Color: _____

    Size and Number Spools: _____

BATTING NEEDED:

    Size: _____

OTHER MATERIALS:

_____

_____

_____

_____

_____

_____

_____

_____

_____

Quilt History

Project / Quilt Name: _____

Date Quilt Top Was Started: _____

Date Quilt Top Was Completed: _____

How Was It Quilted and by whom: _____

Date Quilt was Completed: _____

_____

PHOTO OF THE FINISHED QUILT

Let's Get Started

Date: _____

Who is my quilt for? _____

Why am I making this quilt - will I keep it or gift it? _____

Who will I gift it to? _____

What size quilt? Baby   Twin   Queen   King   Cal King

What is the Pattern Name, if any ? _____

What colors do I want to use? _____

What pattern(s) will I use? _____

What type of batting will I use? _____

Will I hand quilt, machine quilt or hire someone to quilt? _____

Notes: _____
_____
_____
_____
_____
_____
_____
_____
_____
_____
_____
_____
_____
_____
_____
_____
_____

Tables to Help You Calculate Yardage

Keep These Tips In Mind:

Most Quilt Fabrics are 45" wide with about 40" usable.

Divide number of total inches by 36 (number of inches in a yard) to get the number of yards. Add additional yardage to cover for errors.

Don't forget about your binding yardage.

Conversion Decimal to Fraction

Decimal	Fraction
.0625	1/16
.125	1/8
.1875	3/16
.25	1/4
.3125	5/16
.4375	7/16
.5	1/2
.5625	9/16
.625	5/8
.666	2/3
.6875	11/16
.75	3/4
.8125	13/16
.875	7/8
.9375	15/16

Standard Bed Sizes

Bed	Dimensions Inches	Quilt with 16" drop on each side	Std. Batting Sizes
Crib	28" X 52"	60" X 84"	45" X 60"
Twin	39" X 75"	71" X 107"	72" X 90"
Long Twin	39" X 80"	71" X 112"	-----------
Full	54" X 75"	86" X 107"	81" x 96"
Queen	60" X 80"	92" X 112"	90" X 108"
King	76" X 80"	108" X 112"	120" X 120"
California King	72" X 84"	104" X 116"	120" X 120"

Notes

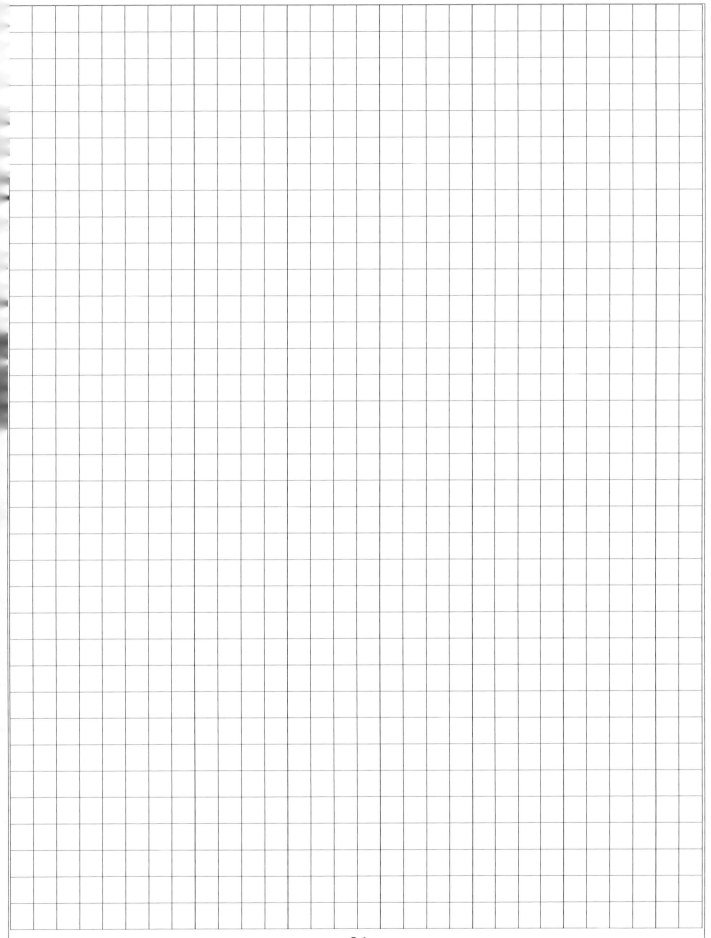

Fabric Swatches and Yardage:

Name of Fabric: _____

Cost Per Yard: _____

Notes: _____

Name of Fabric: _____

Cost Per Yard: _____

Notes: _____

Name of Fabric: _____

Cost Per Yard: _____

Notes: _____

Name of Fabric: _____

Cost Per Yard: _____

Notes: _____

Fabric Swatches and Yardage:

Name of Fabric: _____

Cost Per Yard: _____

Notes: _____

Name of Fabric: _____

Cost Per Yard: _____

Notes: _____

Name of Fabric: _____

Cost Per Yard: _____

Notes: _____

Name of Fabric: _____

Cost Per Yard: _____

Notes: _____

Materials Needed

FABRICS:

Face Fabric: _____
      Light: _____
      Medium: _____
      Dark: _____
Muslin / Backing _____
Binding/Sashing to Go Around Edges _____

THREAD NEEDED:

Color: _____
Size and Number Spools: _____
_____

Color: _____
Size and Number Spools: _____
_____

Color: _____
Size and Number Spools: _____

BATTING NEEDED:

Size: _____

OTHER MATERIALS:

_____
_____
_____
_____
_____
_____
_____
_____
_____
_____

Quilt History

Project / Quilt Name: ————————————————————————————

Date Quilt Top Was Started: ———————————————————————

Date Quilt Top Was Completed: ——————————————————————

How Was It Quilted and by whom: ————————————————————

Date Quilt was Completed: ——————————————————————————

——

PHOTO OF THE FINISHED QUILT

Let's Get Started

Date: _____

Who is my quilt for? _____

Why am I making this quilt - will I keep it or gift it? _____

Who will I gift it to? _____

What size quilt? Baby   Twin   Queen   King   Cal King

What is the Pattern Name, if any ? _____

What colors do I want to use? _____

What pattern(s) will I use? _____

What type of batting will I use? _____

Will I hand quilt, machine quilt or hire someone to quilt? _____

Notes: _____
_____
_____
_____
_____
_____
_____
_____
_____
_____
_____
_____
_____
_____
_____
_____

Tables to Help You Calculate Yardage

Keep These Tips In Mind:

Most Quilt Fabrics are 45" wide with about 40" usable.

Divide number of total inches by 36 (number of inches in a yard) to get the number of yards. Add additional yardage to cover for errors.

Don't forget about your binding yardage.

Conversion Decimal to Fraction

Decimal	Fraction
.0625	1/16
.125	1/8
.1875	3/16
.25	1/4
.3125	5/16
.4375	7/16
.5	1/2
.5625	9/16
.625	5/8
.666	2/3
.6875	11/16
.75	3/4
.8125	13/16
.875	7/8
.9375	15/16

Standard Bed Sizes

Bed	Dimensions Inches	Quilt with 16" drop on each side	Std. Batting Sizes
Crib	28" X 52"	60" X 84"	45" X 60"
Twin	39" X 75"	71" X 107"	72" X 90"
Long Twin	39" X 80"	71" X 112"	-----------
Full	54" X 75"	86" X 107"	81" x 96"
Queen	60" X 80"	92" X 112"	90" X 108"
King	76" X 80"	108" X 112"	120" X 120"
California King	72" X 84"	104" X 116"	120" X 120"

Notes

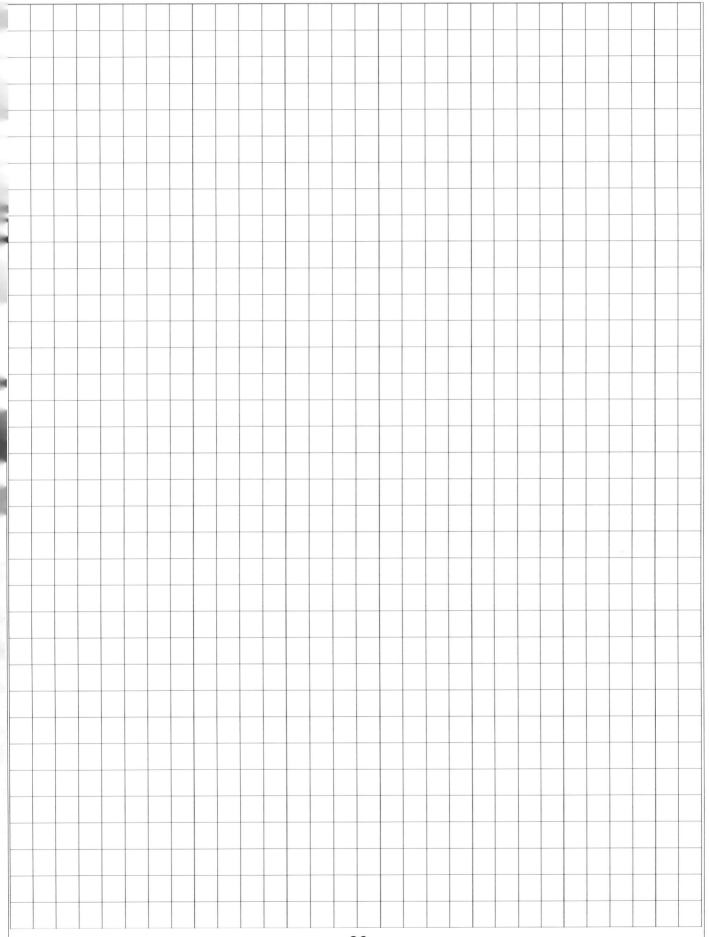

Fabric Swatches and Yardage:

Name of Fabric: _____

Cost Per Yard: _____

Notes: _____

Name of Fabric: _____

Cost Per Yard: _____

Notes: _____

Name of Fabric: _____

Cost Per Yard: _____

Notes: _____

Name of Fabric: _____

Cost Per Yard: _____

Notes: _____

Fabric Swatches and Yardage:

Name of Fabric: _____

Cost Per Yard: _____

Notes: _____

Name of Fabric: _____

Cost Per Yard: _____

Notes: _____

Name of Fabric: _____

Cost Per Yard: _____

Notes: _____

Name of Fabric: _____

Cost Per Yard: _____

Notes: _____

Materials Needed

FABRICS:

Face Fabric: _____
   Light: _____
   Medium: _____
   Dark: _____
Muslin / Backing _____
Binding/Sashing to Go Around Edges _____

THREAD NEEDED:

Color: _____
Size and Number Spools: _____
_____
Color: _____
Size and Number Spools: _____
_____
Color: _____
Size and Number Spools: _____

BATTING NEEDED:

Size: _____

OTHER MATERIALS:

_____
_____
_____
_____
_____
_____
_____
_____
_____

Quilt History

Project / Quilt Name: _____

Date Quilt Top Was Started: _____

Date Quilt Top Was Completed: _____

How Was It Quilted and by whom: _____

Date Quilt was Completed: _____

_____

PHOTO OF THE FINISHED QUILT

Let's Get Started

Date: _____

Who is my quilt for? _____

Why am I making this quilt - will I keep it or gift it? _____

Who will I gift it to? _____

What size quilt? Baby   Twin   Queen   King   Cal King

What is the Pattern Name, if any ? _____

What colors do I want to use? _____

What pattern(s) will I use? _____

What type of batting will I use? _____

Will I hand quilt, machine quilt or hire someone to quilt? _____

Notes: _____
_____
_____
_____
_____
_____
_____
_____
_____
_____
_____
_____
_____
_____
_____
_____

Tables to Help You Calculate Yardage

Keep These Tips In Mind:

Most Quilt Fabrics are 45" wide with about 40" usable.

Divide number of total inches by 36 (number of inches in a yard) to get the number of yards. Add additional yardage to cover for errors.

Don't forget about your binding yardage.

Conversion Decimal to Fraction

Decimal	Fraction
.0625	1/16
.125	1/8
.1875	3/16
.25	1/4
.3125	5/16
.4375	7/16
.5	1/2
.5625	9/16
.625	5/8
.666	2/3
.6875	11/16
.75	3/4
.8125	13/16
.875	7/8
.9375	15/16

Standard Bed Sizes

Bed	Dimensions Inches	Quilt with 16" drop on each side	Std. Batting Sizes
Crib	28" X 52"	60" X 84"	45" X 60"
Twin	39" X 75"	71" X 107"	72" X 90"
Long Twin	39" X 80"	71" X 112"	-----------
Full	54" X 75"	86" X 107"	81" x 96"
Queen	60" X 80"	92" X 112"	90" X 108"
King	76" X 80"	108" X 112"	120" X 120"
California King	72" X 84"	104" X 116"	120" X 120"

Notes

Fabric Swatches and Yardage:

Name of Fabric: _____

Cost Per Yard: _____

Notes: _____

Name of Fabric: _____

Cost Per Yard: _____

Notes: _____

Name of Fabric: _____

Cost Per Yard: _____

Notes: _____

Name of Fabric: _____

Cost Per Yard: _____

Notes: _____

Fabric Swatches and Yardage:

Name of Fabric: _____

Cost Per Yard: _____

Notes: _____

Name of Fabric: _____

Cost Per Yard: _____

Notes: _____

Name of Fabric: _____

Cost Per Yard: _____

Notes: _____

Name of Fabric: _____

Cost Per Yard: _____

Notes: _____

Materials Needed

FABRICS:

    Face Fabric: _____

        Light: _____

        Medium: _____

        Dark: _____

    Muslin / Backing _____

    Binding/Sashing to Go Around Edges _____

THREAD NEEDED:

    Color: _____

    Size and Number Spools: _____

    _____

    Color: _____

    Size and Number Spools: _____

    _____

    Color: _____

    Size and Number Spools: _____

BATTING NEEDED:

    Size: _____

OTHER MATERIALS:

_____

_____

_____

_____

_____

_____

_____

_____

_____

Quilt History

Project / Quilt Name: _____

Date Quilt Top Was Started: _____

Date Quilt Top Was Completed: _____

How Was It Quilted and by whom: _____

Date Quilt was Completed: _____

_____

PHOTO OF THE FINISHED QUILT

Let's Get Started

Date: _____

Who is my quilt for? _____

Why am I making this quilt - will I keep it or gift it? _____

Who will I gift it to? _____

What size quilt? Baby   Twin   Queen   King   Cal King

What is the Pattern Name, if any ? _____

What colors do I want to use? _____

What pattern(s) will I use? _____

What type of batting will I use? _____

Will I hand quilt, machine quilt or hire someone to quilt? _____

Notes: _____
_____
_____
_____
_____
_____
_____
_____
_____
_____
_____
_____
_____
_____
_____
_____

Tables to Help You Calculate Yardage

Keep These Tips In Mind:

Most Quilt Fabrics are 45" wide with about 40" usable.

Divide number of total inches by 36 (number of inches in a yard) to get the number of yards. Add additional yardage to cover for errors.

Don't forget about your binding yardage.

Conversion Decimal to Fraction

Decimal	Fraction
.0625	1/16
.125	1/8
.1875	3/16
.25	1/4
.3125	5/16
.4375	7/16
.5	1/2
.5625	9/16
.625	5/8
.666	2/3
.6875	11/16
.75	3/4
.8125	13/16
.875	7/8
.9375	15/16

Standard Bed Sizes

Bed	Dimensions Inches	Quilt with 16" drop on each side	Std. Batting Sizes
Crib	28" X 52"	60" X 84"	45" X 60"
Twin	39" X 75"	71" X 107"	72" X 90"
Long Twin	39" X 80"	71" X 112"	-----------
Full	54" X 75"	86" X 107"	81" x 96"
Queen	60" X 80"	92" X 112"	90" X 108"
King	76" X 80"	108" X 112"	120" X 120"
California King	72" X 84"	104" X 116"	120" X 120"

Notes

Fabric Swatches and Yardage:

Name of Fabric: _____

Cost Per Yard: _____

Notes: _____

Name of Fabric: _____

Cost Per Yard: _____

Notes: _____

Name of Fabric: _____

Cost Per Yard: _____

Notes: _____

Name of Fabric: _____

Cost Per Yard: _____

Notes: _____

Fabric Swatches and Yardage:

Name of Fabric: _____
_____
Cost Per Yard: _____
_____
Notes: _____
_____

Name of Fabric: _____
_____
Cost Per Yard: _____
_____
Notes: _____
_____

Name of Fabric: _____
_____
Cost Per Yard: _____
_____
Notes: _____
_____

Name of Fabric: _____
_____
Cost Per Yard: _____
_____
Notes: _____
_____

Materials Needed

FABRICS:

Face Fabric: _____
       Light: _____
       Medium: _____
       Dark: _____
Muslin / Backing _____
Binding/Sashing to Go Around Edges _____

THREAD NEEDED:

Color: _____
Size and Number Spools: _____
_____

Color: _____
Size and Number Spools: _____
_____

Color: _____
Size and Number Spools: _____

BATTING NEEDED:

Size: _____

OTHER MATERIALS:

_____
_____
_____
_____
_____
_____
_____
_____
_____
_____

Quilt History

Project / Quilt Name: _____

Date Quilt Top Was Started: _____

Date Quilt Top Was Completed: _____

How Was It Quilted and by whom: _____

Date Quilt was Completed: _____

_____

PHOTO OF THE FINISHED QUILT

Let's Get Started

Date: _____

Who is my quilt for? _____

Why am I making this quilt - will I keep it or gift it? _____

Who will I gift it to? _____

What size quilt? Baby   Twin   Queen   King   Cal King

What is the Pattern Name, if any ? _____

What colors do I want to use? _____

What pattern(s) will I use? _____

What type of batting will I use? _____

Will I hand quilt, machine quilt or hire someone to quilt? _____

Notes: _____
_____
_____
_____
_____
_____
_____
_____
_____
_____
_____
_____
_____
_____
_____
_____
_____

Tables to Help You Calculate Yardage

Keep These Tips In Mind:

Most Quilt Fabrics are 45" wide with about 40" usable.

Divide number of total inches by 36 (number of inches in a yard) to get the number of yards. Add additional yardage to cover for errors.

Don't forget about your binding yardage.

Conversion Decimal to Fraction

Decimal	Fraction
.0625	1/16
.125	1/8
.1875	3/16
.25	1/4
.3125	5/16
.4375	7/16
.5	1/2
.5625	9/16
.625	5/8
.666	2/3
.6875	11/16
.75	3/4
.8125	13/16
.875	7/8
.9375	15/16

Standard Bed Sizes

Bed	Dimensions Inches	Quilt with 16" drop on each side	Std. Batting Sizes
Crib	28" X 52"	60" X 84"	45" X 60"
Twin	39" X 75"	71" X 107"	72" X 90"
Long Twin	39" X 80"	71" X 112"	-----------
Full	54" X 75"	86" X 107"	81" x 96"
Queen	60" X 80"	92" X 112"	90" X 108"
King	76" X 80"	108" X 112"	120" X 120"
California King	72" X 84"	104" X 116"	120" X 120"

Notes

Fabric Swatches and Yardage:

Name of Fabric: _____

Cost Per Yard: _____

Notes: _____

Name of Fabric: _____

Cost Per Yard: _____

Notes: _____

Name of Fabric: _____

Cost Per Yard: _____

Notes: _____

Name of Fabric: _____

Cost Per Yard: _____

Notes: _____

Fabric Swatches and Yardage:

Name of Fabric: _____
_____

Cost Per Yard: _____
_____

Notes: _____
_____

Name of Fabric: _____
_____

Cost Per Yard: _____
_____

Notes: _____
_____

Name of Fabric: _____
_____

Cost Per Yard: _____
_____

Notes: _____
_____

Name of Fabric: _____
_____

Cost Per Yard: _____
_____

Notes: _____
_____

Materials Needed

FABRICS:

    Face Fabric: _____
        Light: _____
        Medium: _____
        Dark: _____
    Muslin / Backing _____
    Binding/Sashing to Go Around Edges _____

THREAD NEEDED:

    Color: _____
    Size and Number Spools: _____
    _____
    Color: _____
    Size and Number Spools: _____
    _____
    Color: _____
    Size and Number Spools: _____

BATTING NEEDED:

    Size: _____

OTHER MATERIALS:

_____
_____
_____
_____
_____
_____
_____
_____
_____
_____

Quilt History

Project / Quilt Name: _____

Date Quilt Top Was Started: _____

Date Quilt Top Was Completed: _____

How Was It Quilted and by whom: _____

Date Quilt was Completed: _____

_____

PHOTO OF THE FINISHED QUILT

Let's Get Started

Date: _____

Who is my quilt for? _____

Why am I making this quilt - will I keep it or gift it? _____

Who will I gift it to? _____

What size quilt? Baby   Twin   Queen   King   Cal King

What is the Pattern Name, if any ? _____

What colors do I want to use? _____

What pattern(s) will I use? _____

What type of batting will I use? _____

Will I hand quilt, machine quilt or hire someone to quilt? ____

Notes: _____
_____
_____
_____
_____
_____
_____
_____
_____
_____
_____
_____
_____
_____
_____
_____
_____

Tables to Help You Calculate Yardage

Keep These Tips In Mind:

Most Quilt Fabrics are 45" wide with about 40" usable.

Divide number of total inches by 36 (number of inches in a yard) to get the number of yards. Add additional yardage to cover for errors.

Don't forget about your binding yardage.

Conversion Decimal to Fraction

Decimal	Fraction
.0625	1/16
.125	1/8
.1875	3/16
.25	1/4
.3125	5/16
.4375	7/16
.5	1/2
.5625	9/16
.625	5/8
.666	2/3
.6875	11/16
.75	3/4
.8125	13/16
.875	7/8
.9375	15/16

Standard Bed Sizes

Bed	Dimensions Inches	Quilt with 16" drop on each side	Std. Batting Sizes
Crib	28" X 52"	60" X 84"	45" X 60"
Twin	39" X 75"	71" X 107"	72" X 90"
Long Twin	39" X 80"	71" X 112"	-----------
Full	54" X 75"	86" X 107"	81" x 96"
Queen	60" X 80"	92" X 112"	90" X 108"
King	76" X 80"	108" X 112"	120" X 120"
California King	72" X 84"	104" X 116"	120" X 120"

Notes

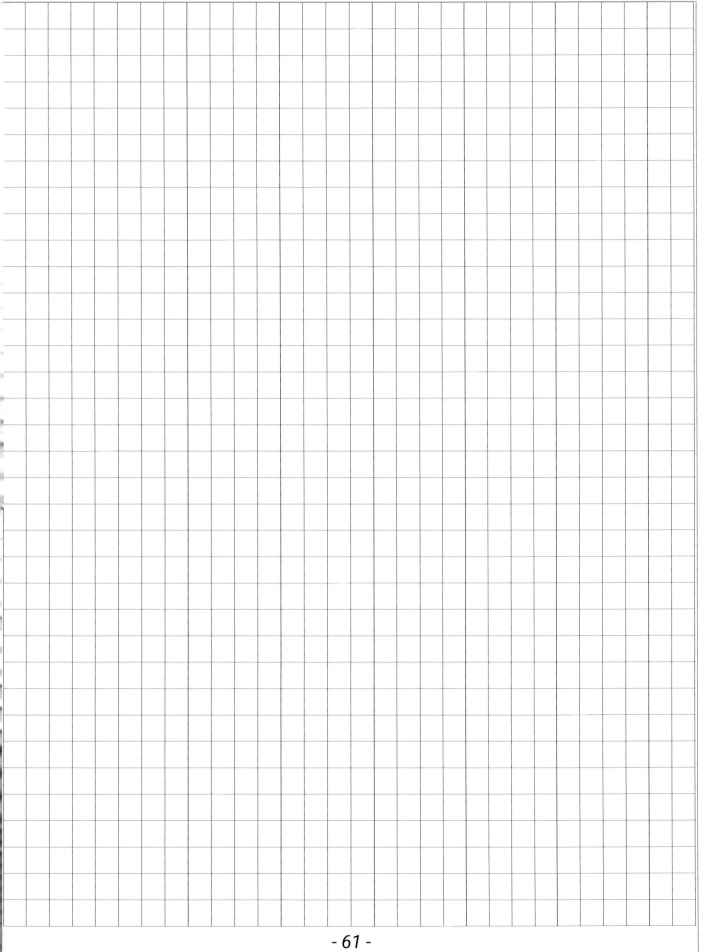

Fabric Swatches and Yardage:

Name of Fabric: _____

Cost Per Yard: _____

Notes: _____

Name of Fabric: _____

Cost Per Yard: _____

Notes: _____

Name of Fabric: _____

Cost Per Yard: _____

Notes: _____

Name of Fabric: _____

Cost Per Yard: _____

Notes: _____

Fabric Swatches and Yardage:

Name of Fabric: _____

Cost Per Yard: _____

Notes: _____

Name of Fabric: _____

Cost Per Yard: _____

Notes: _____

Name of Fabric: _____

Cost Per Yard: _____

Notes: _____

Name of Fabric: _____

Cost Per Yard: _____

Notes: _____

Materials Needed

FABRICS:

Face Fabric: _____
    Light: _____
    Medium: _____
    Dark: _____
Muslin / Backing _____
Binding/Sashing to Go Around Edges _____

THREAD NEEDED:

Color: _____
Size and Number Spools: _____
_____

Color: _____
Size and Number Spools: _____
_____

Color: _____
Size and Number Spools: _____

BATTING NEEDED:

Size: _____

OTHER MATERIALS:

_____
_____
_____
_____
_____
_____
_____
_____
_____

Quilt History

Project / Quilt Name: ─────────────────────────────

Date Quilt Top Was Started: ─────────────────────────

Date Quilt Top Was Completed: ───────────────────────

How Was It Quilted and by whom: ─────────────────────

Date Quilt was Completed: ────────────────────────────

───

PHOTO OF THE FINISHED QUILT

Let's Get Started

Date: _____

Who is my quilt for? _____

Why am I making this quilt - will I keep it or gift it? _____

Who will I gift it to? _____

What size quilt?   Baby   Twin   Queen   King   Cal King

What is the Pattern Name, if any ? _____

What colors do I want to use? _____

What pattern(s) will I use? _____

What type of batting will I use? _____

Will I hand quilt, machine quilt or hire someone to quilt? _____

Notes: _____
_____
_____
_____
_____
_____
_____
_____
_____
_____
_____
_____
_____
_____
_____
_____

Tables to Help You Calculate Yardage

Keep These Tips In Mind:

Most Quilt Fabrics are 45" wide with about 40" usable.

Divide number of total inches by 36 (number of inches in a yard) to get the number of yards. Add additional yardage to cover for errors.

Don't forget about your binding yardage.

Conversion Decimal to Fraction

Decimal	Fraction
.0625	1/16
.125	1/8
.1875	3/16
.25	1/4
.3125	5/16
.4375	7/16
.5	1/2
.5625	9/16
.625	5/8
.666	2/3
.6875	11/16
.75	3/4
.8125	13/16
.875	7/8
.9375	15/16

Standard Bed Sizes

Bed	Dimensions Inches	Quilt with 16" drop on each side	Std. Batting Sizes
Crib	28" X 52"	60" X 84"	45" X 60"
Twin	39" X 75"	71" X 107"	72" X 90"
Long Twin	39" X 80"	71" X 112"	-----------
Full	54" X 75"	86" X 107"	81" x 96"
Queen	60" X 80"	92" X 112"	90" X 108"
King	76" X 80"	108" X 112"	120" X 120"
California King	72" X 84"	104" X 116"	120" X 120"

Notes

Fabric Swatches and Yardage:

Name of Fabric: _____

Cost Per Yard: _____

Notes: _____

Name of Fabric: _____

Cost Per Yard: _____

Notes: _____

Name of Fabric: _____

Cost Per Yard: _____

Notes: _____

Name of Fabric: _____

Cost Per Yard: _____

Notes: _____

Fabric Swatches and Yardage:

Name of Fabric: _____

Cost Per Yard: _____

Notes: _____

Name of Fabric: _____

Cost Per Yard: _____

Notes: _____

Name of Fabric: _____

Cost Per Yard: _____

Notes: _____

Name of Fabric: _____

Cost Per Yard: _____

Notes: _____

Materials Needed

FABRICS:

    Face Fabric: _____

        Light: _____

        Medium: _____

        Dark: _____

    Muslin / Backing _____

    Binding/Sashing to Go Around Edges _____

THREAD NEEDED:

    Color: _____

    Size and Number Spools: _____

    _____

    Color: _____

    Size and Number Spools: _____

    _____

    Color: _____

    Size and Number Spools: _____

BATTING NEEDED:

    Size: _____

OTHER MATERIALS:

_____

_____

_____

_____

_____

_____

_____

_____

_____

Quilt History

Project / Quilt Name: ——————————————————————

Date Quilt Top Was Started: ——————————————————

Date Quilt Top Was Completed: ——————————————————

How Was It Quilted and by whom: ——————————————————

Date Quilt was Completed: ——————————————————————

————————————————————————————————————

PHOTO OF THE FINISHED QUILT

Let's Get Started

Date: _____

Who is my quilt for? _____

Why am I making this quilt - will I keep it or gift it? _____

Who will I gift it to? _____

What size quilt? Baby   Twin   Queen   King   Cal King

What is the Pattern Name, if any ? _____

What colors do I want to use? _____

What pattern(s) will I use? _____

What type of batting will I use? _____

Will I hand quilt, machine quilt or hire someone to quilt? _____

Notes: _____
_____
_____
_____
_____
_____
_____
_____
_____
_____
_____
_____
_____
_____
_____
_____
_____

Tables to Help You Calculate Yardage

Keep These Tips In Mind:

Most Quilt Fabrics are 45" wide with about 40" usable.

Divide number of total inches by 36 (number of inches in a yard) to get the number of yards. Add additional yardage to cover for errors.

Don't forget about your binding yardage.

Conversion Decimal to Fraction

Decimal	Fraction
.0625	1/16
.125	1/8
.1875	3/16
.25	1/4
.3125	5/16
.4375	7/16
.5	1/2
.5625	9/16
.625	5/8
.666	2/3
.6875	11/16
.75	3/4
.8125	13/16
.875	7/8
.9375	15/16

Standard Bed Sizes

Bed	Dimensions Inches	Quilt with 16" drop on each side	Std. Batting Sizes
Crib	28" X 52"	60" X 84"	45" X 60"
Twin	39" X 75"	71" X 107"	72" X 90"
Long Twin	39" X 80"	71" X 112"	-----------
Full	54" X 75"	86" X 107"	81" x 96"
Queen	60" X 80"	92" X 112"	90" X 108"
King	76" X 80"	108" X 112"	120" X 120"
California King	72" X 84"	104" X 116"	120" X 120"

Notes

Fabric Swatches and Yardage:

Name of Fabric: _____

Cost Per Yard: _____

Notes: _____

Name of Fabric: _____

Cost Per Yard: _____

Notes: _____

Name of Fabric: _____

Cost Per Yard: _____

Notes: _____

Name of Fabric: _____

Cost Per Yard: _____

Notes: _____

Fabric Swatches and Yardage:

Name of Fabric: _____

Cost Per Yard: _____

Notes: _____

Name of Fabric: _____

Cost Per Yard: _____

Notes: _____

Name of Fabric: _____

Cost Per Yard: _____

Notes: _____

Name of Fabric: _____

Cost Per Yard: _____

Notes: _____

Materials Needed

FABRICS:

Face Fabric: _____
       Light: _____
       Medium: _____
       Dark: _____
Muslin / Backing _____
Binding/Sashing to Go Around Edges _____

THREAD NEEDED:

Color: _____
Size and Number Spools: _____
_____
Color: _____
Size and Number Spools: _____
_____
Color: _____
Size and Number Spools: _____

BATTING NEEDED:

Size: _____

OTHER MATERIALS:

_____
_____
_____
_____
_____
_____
_____
_____
_____

Quilt History

Project / Quilt Name: _____

Date Quilt Top Was Started: _____

Date Quilt Top Was Completed: _____

How Was It Quilted and by whom: _____

Date Quilt was Completed: _____

_____

PHOTO OF THE FINISHED QUILT

Let's Get Started

Date: _____

Who is my quilt for? _____

Why am I making this quilt - will I keep it or gift it? _____

Who will I gift it to? _____

What size quilt? Baby   Twin   Queen   King   Cal King

What is the Pattern Name, if any ? _____

What colors do I want to use? _____

What pattern(s) will I use? _____

What type of batting will I use? _____

Will I hand quilt, machine quilt or hire someone to quilt? _____

Notes: _____
_____
_____
_____
_____
_____
_____
_____
_____
_____
_____
_____
_____
_____
_____
_____
_____

Tables to Help You Calculate Yardage

Keep These Tips In Mind:

Most Quilt Fabrics are 45" wide with about 40" usable.

Divide number of total inches by 36 (number of inches in a yard) to get the number of yards. Add additional yardage to cover for errors.

Don't forget about your binding yardage.

Conversion Decimal to Fraction

Decimal	Fraction
.0625	1/16
.125	1/8
.1875	3/16
.25	1/4
.3125	5/16
.4375	7/16
.5	1/2
.5625	9/16
.625	5/8
.666	2/3
.6875	11/16
.75	3/4
.8125	13/16
.875	7/8
.9375	15/16

Standard Bed Sizes

Bed	Dimensions Inches	Quilt with 16" drop on each side	Std. Batting Sizes
Crib	28" X 52"	60" X 84"	45" X 60"
Twin	39" X 75"	71" X 107"	72" X 90"
Long Twin	39" X 80"	71" X 112"	-----------
Full	54" X 75"	86" X 107"	81" x 96"
Queen	60" X 80"	92" X 112"	90" X 108"
King	76" X 80"	108" X 112"	120" X 120"
California King	72" X 84"	104" X 116"	120" X 120"

Notes

Fabric Swatches and Yardage:

Name of Fabric: _____

Cost Per Yard: _____

Notes: _____

Name of Fabric: _____

Cost Per Yard: _____

Notes: _____

Name of Fabric: _____

Cost Per Yard: _____

Notes: _____

Name of Fabric: _____

Cost Per Yard: _____

Notes: _____

Fabric Swatches and Yardage:

Name of Fabric: _____
_____
Cost Per Yard: _____
_____
Notes: _____
_____

Name of Fabric: _____
_____
Cost Per Yard: _____
_____
Notes: _____
_____

Name of Fabric: _____
_____
Cost Per Yard: _____
_____
Notes: _____
_____

Name of Fabric: _____
_____
Cost Per Yard: _____
_____
Notes: _____
_____

Materials Needed

FABRICS:

    Face Fabric: _____

        Light: _____

        Medium: _____

        Dark: _____

    Muslin / Backing _____

    Binding/Sashing to Go Around Edges _____

THREAD NEEDED:

    Color: _____

    Size and Number Spools: _____

    _____

    Color: _____

    Size and Number Spools: _____

    _____

    Color: _____

    Size and Number Spools: _____

BATTING NEEDED:

    Size: _____

OTHER MATERIALS:

_____

_____

_____

_____

_____

_____

_____

_____

_____

Quilt History

Project / Quilt Name: _____

Date Quilt Top Was Started: _____

Date Quilt Top Was Completed: _____

How Was It Quilted and by whom: _____

Date Quilt was Completed: _____

_____

PHOTO OF THE FINISHED QUILT

Let's Get Started

Date: _____

Who is my quilt for? _____

Why am I making this quilt - will I keep it or gift it? _____

Who will I gift it to? _____

What size quilt? Baby   Twin   Queen   King   Cal King

What is the Pattern Name, if any ? _____

What colors do I want to use? _____

What pattern(s) will I use? _____

What type of batting will I use? _____

Will I hand quilt, machine quilt or hire someone to quilt? _____

Notes: _____
_____
_____
_____
_____
_____
_____
_____
_____
_____
_____
_____
_____
_____
_____
_____
_____
_____
_____

Tables to Help You Calculate Yardage

Keep These Tips In Mind:

Most Quilt Fabrics are 45" wide with about 40" usable.

Divide number of total inches by 36 (number of inches in a yard) to get the number of yards. Add additional yardage to cover for errors.

Don't forget about your binding yardage.

Conversion Decimal to Fraction

Decimal	Fraction
.0625	1/16
.125	1/8
.1875	3/16
.25	1/4
.3125	5/16
.4375	7/16
.5	1/2
.5625	9/16
.625	5/8
.666	2/3
.6875	11/16
.75	3/4
.8125	13/16
.875	7/8
.9375	15/16

Standard Bed Sizes

Bed	Dimensions Inches	Quilt with 16" drop on each side	Std. Batting Sizes
Crib	28" X 52"	60" X 84"	45" X 60"
Twin	39" X 75"	71" X 107"	72" X 90"
Long Twin	39" X 80"	71" X 112"	-----------
Full	54" X 75"	86" X 107"	81" x 96"
Queen	60" X 80"	92" X 112"	90" X 108"
King	76" X 80"	108" X 112"	120" X 120"
California King	72" X 84"	104" X 116"	120" X 120"

Notes

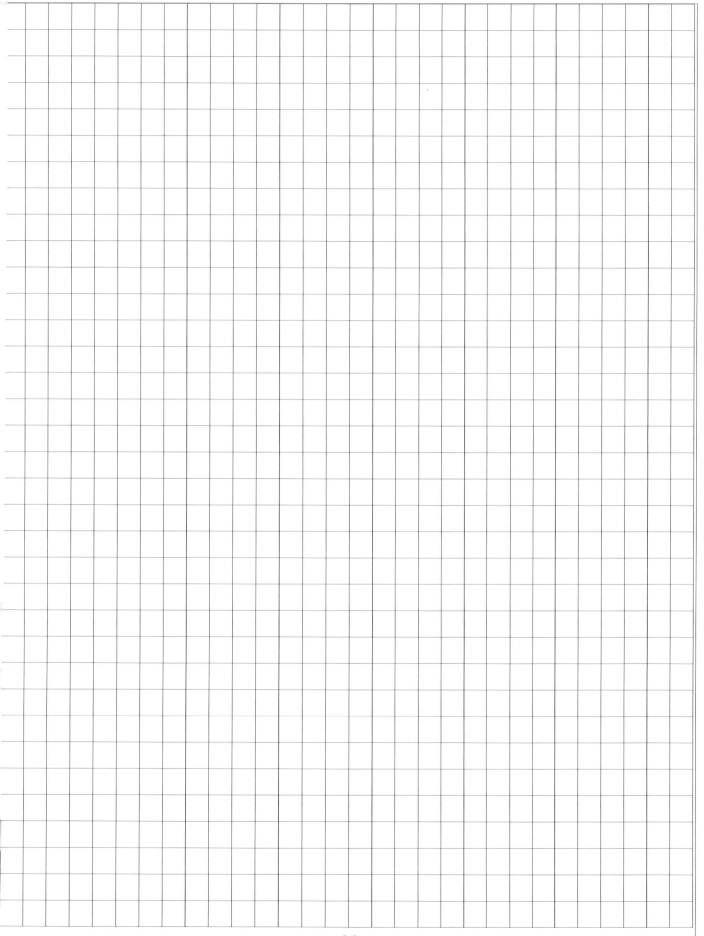

Fabric Swatches and Yardage:

Name of Fabric: _____

Cost Per Yard: _____

Notes: _____

Name of Fabric: _____

Cost Per Yard: _____

Notes: _____

Name of Fabric: _____

Cost Per Yard: _____

Notes: _____

Name of Fabric: _____

Cost Per Yard: _____

Notes: _____

Fabric Swatches and Yardage:

Name of Fabric: _____

_____

Cost Per Yard: _____

_____

Notes: _____

_____

Name of Fabric: _____

_____

Cost Per Yard: _____

_____

Notes: _____

_____

Name of Fabric: _____

_____

Cost Per Yard: _____

_____

Notes: _____

_____

Name of Fabric: _____

_____

Cost Per Yard: _____

_____

Notes: _____

_____

Materials Needed

FABRICS:

    Face Fabric: _____
        Light: _____
        Medium: _____
        Dark: _____
    Muslin / Backing _____
    Binding/Sashing to Go Around Edges _____

THREAD NEEDED:

    Color: _____
    Size and Number Spools: _____
    _____

    Color: _____
    Size and Number Spools: _____
    _____

    Color: _____
    Size and Number Spools: _____

BATTING NEEDED:

    Size: _____

OTHER MATERIALS:

_____
_____
_____
_____
_____
_____
_____
_____
_____
_____

Quilt History

Project / Quilt Name: ─────────────────────────

Date Quilt Top Was Started: ─────────────────────

Date Quilt Top Was Completed: ───────────────────

How Was It Quilted and by whom: ─────────────────

Date Quilt was Completed: ────────────────────────

───

PHOTO OF THE FINISHED QUILT

Let's Get Started

Date: _____

Who is my quilt for? _____

Why am I making this quilt - will I keep it or gift it? _____

Who will I gift it to? _____

What size quilt? Baby   Twin   Queen   King   Cal King

What is the Pattern Name, if any ? _____

What colors do I want to use? _____

What pattern(s) will I use? _____

What type of batting will I use? _____

Will I hand quilt, machine quilt or hire someone to quilt? _____

Notes: _____
_____
_____
_____
_____
_____
_____
_____
_____
_____
_____
_____
_____
_____
_____
_____
_____
_____

Tables to Help You Calculate Yardage

Keep These Tips In Mind:

Most Quilt Fabrics are 45" wide with about 40" usable.

Divide number of total inches by 36 (number of inches in a yard) to get the number of yards. Add additional yardage to cover for errors.

Don't forget about your binding yardage.

Conversion Decimal to Fraction

Decimal	Fraction
.0625	1/16
.125	1/8
.1875	3/16
.25	1/4
.3125	5/16
.4375	7/16
.5	1/2
.5625	9/16
.625	5/8
.666	2/3
.6875	11/16
.75	3/4
.8125	13/16
.875	7/8
.9375	15/16

Standard Bed Sizes

Bed	Dimensions Inches	Quilt with 16" drop on each side	Std. Batting Sizes
Crib	28" X 52"	60" X 84"	45" X 60"
Twin	39" X 75"	71" X 107"	72" X 90"
Long Twin	39" X 80"	71" X 112"	-----------
Full	54" X 75"	86" X 107"	81" x 96"
Queen	60" X 80"	92" X 112"	90" X 108"
King	76" X 80"	108" X 112"	120" X 120"
California King	72" X 84"	104" X 116"	120" X 120"

Notes

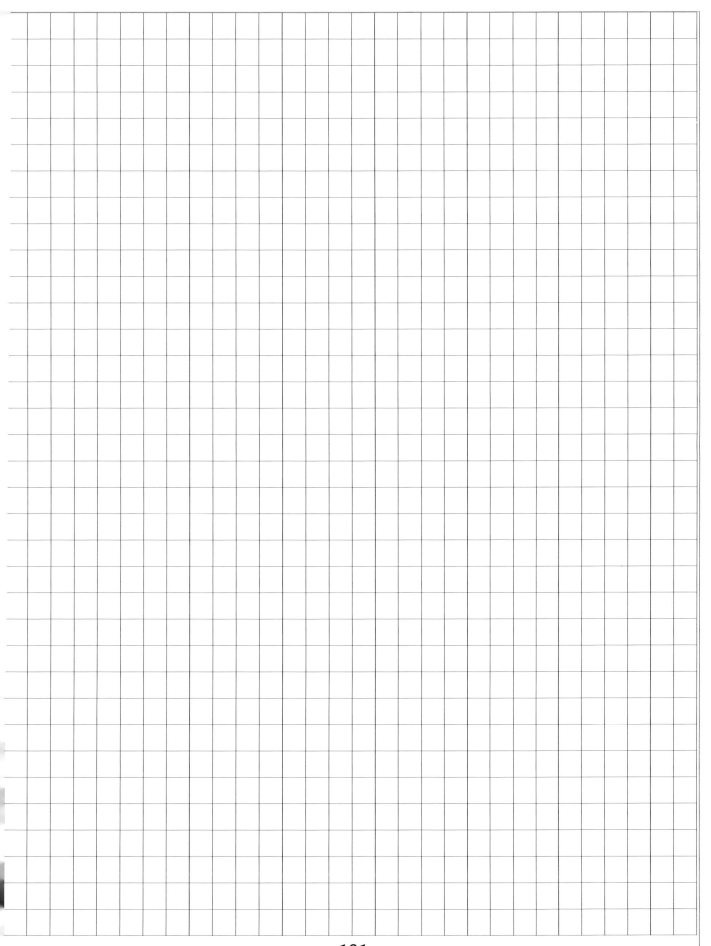

Fabric Swatches and Yardage:

Name of Fabric: _____

Cost Per Yard: _____

Notes: _____

Name of Fabric: _____

Cost Per Yard: _____

Notes: _____

Name of Fabric: _____

Cost Per Yard: _____

Notes: _____

Name of Fabric: _____

Cost Per Yard: _____

Notes: _____

Fabric Swatches and Yardage:

Name of Fabric: _____

Cost Per Yard: _____

Notes: _____

Name of Fabric: _____

Cost Per Yard: _____

Notes: _____

Name of Fabric: _____

Cost Per Yard: _____

Notes: _____

Name of Fabric: _____

Cost Per Yard: _____

Notes: _____

Materials Needed

FABRICS:

    Face Fabric: _____
        Light: _____
        Medium: _____
        Dark: _____
    Muslin / Backing _____
    Binding/Sashing to Go Around Edges _____

THREAD NEEDED:

    Color: _____
    Size and Number Spools: _____
    _____

    Color: _____
    Size and Number Spools: _____
    _____

    Color: _____
    Size and Number Spools: _____

BATTING NEEDED:

    Size: _____

OTHER MATERIALS:

_____
_____
_____
_____
_____
_____
_____
_____
_____
_____

Quilt History

Project / Quilt Name: —————————————————————

Date Quilt Top Was Started: —————————————————————

Date Quilt Top Was Completed: —————————————————————

How Was It Quilted and by whom: —————————————————————

Date Quilt was Completed: —————————————————————

—————————————————————

PHOTO OF THE FINISHED QUILT

Date	Quilting Project Name	Page Number

Date	Quilting Project Name	Page Number

Date	Quilting Project Name	Page Number

Date	Quilting Project Name	Page Number

Made in the USA
San Bernardino, CA
01 December 2019